W9-AIA-145

MEASURE UP MATH

TIME

Chris Woodford

Gareth Stevens
Publishing

Please visit our website, www.garethstevens.com. For a free color catalog of all our high-quality books, call toll-free 1-800-542-2595 or fax 1-877-542-2596.

Library of Congress Cataloging-in-Publication Data

Woodford, Chris.
Time / Chris Woodford.
    p. cm. — (Measure up math)
Includes bibliographical references and index.
ISBN 978-1-4339-7454-0 (pbk.)
ISBN 978-1-4339-7455-7 (6-pack)
ISBN 978-1-4339-7453-3 (lib. bdg.)
1. Clocks and watches—Juvenile literature. 2. Time measurements—Juvenile literature. 3. Time—Juvenile literature. I. Title.
TS542.5.W66 2013
681.1'18—dc23

2011052968

Published in 2013 by
Gareth Stevens Publishing
111 East 14th Street, Suite 349
New York, NY 10003

© 2013 Brown Bear Books Ltd

For Brown Bear Books Ltd:
Editorial Director: Lindsey Lowe
Managing Editor: Tim Harris
Children's Publisher: Anne O'Daly
Art Director: Jeni Child
Designer: Lynne Lennon
Picture Manager: Sophie Mortimer
Production Director: Alastair Gourlay

Picture Credits:
Key: t = top, b = bottom
Front Cover: Shutterstock
Interior: NASA: GRIN 20–21; **Shutterstock:** Chandos 11, Franco Mantegani 4–5, Mike Michaels 16–17, Paul Paladin 6, Photos19 10, PhotoSky 12–13, Valery Seleznev 14; **Thinkstock:** Hemera 8–9, 18, 26, istockphoto 18, PhotoObjects.net 17t; **Topfoto:** Keystone 20b. All other artworks and photographs Brown Bear Books.
Brown Bear Books has made every attempt to contact the copyright holder. If anyone has any information could they please contact smortimer@windmillbooks.co.uk

All Artworks © Brown Bear Books Ltd

Manufactured in the United States of America
1 2 3 4 5 6 7 8 9   12 11 10

CPSIA compliance information: Batch #BRS12GS: For further information contact Gareth Stevens, **New York, New York** at 1-800-542-2595.

CONTENTS

WHAT IS TIME?

▶▶▶ **E**ach birthday, you become one year older. You do not get older just on your birthdays, though. You get a little bit older every day. Time is how we mark the rate at which we age. We cannot see time, but it is always there. Although time is invisible, we can measure it with watches, clocks, and calendars.

Earth, Moon, and Sun

Our ideas about time come from the way Earth, the Moon, and the Sun move in the sky. It takes a year for Earth to circle the Sun. It takes about a month for the Moon to move around Earth. All this time, Earth is also spinning very slowly like a top. It takes 24 hours for Earth to spin once.

We feel it is day when our part of Earth faces the Sun and night when our part of Earth faces away from the Sun.

▼ It takes about a month for the Moon to move once around Earth. The Moon's shape appears to change throughout the month. A crescent Moon (below, far left) is a thin slice. A full Moon (below, far right) is a full circle.

FACT

A year usually has 365 days. However, every fourth year has 366 days. It is called a leap year.

▶ PASSING SEASONS

Earth turns around an imaginary line called an axis. The axis leans slightly to one side. As Earth revolves around the Sun, the Northern Hemisphere, or northern half of Earth, tilts toward the Sun at some times of the year (1) and away from the Sun at the other times (2). When the Northern Hemisphere tilts toward the Sun, it has summer because there are more hours of daylight. The Sun also climbs higher in the sky, making the sunlight stronger and warmer.

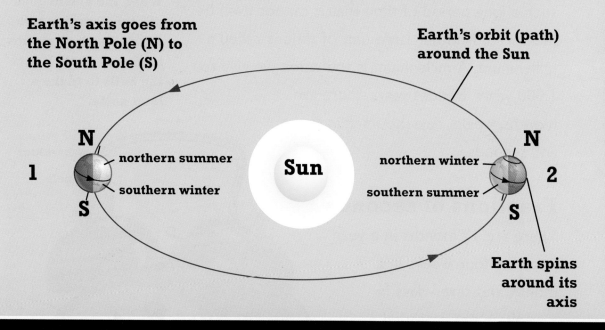

Earth's axis goes from the North Pole (N) to the South Pole (S)

Earth's orbit (path) around the Sun

N

1

northern summer

southern winter

S

Sun

northern winter

southern summer

N

2

S

Earth spins around its axis

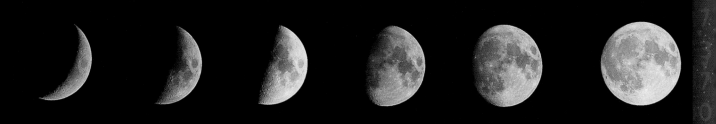

YEARS, DAYS, SECONDS

▶▶▶ **T**ime goes on forever. To make it easier to measure, we divide it into smaller pieces, or units. The biggest unit of time is an eon. An eon is such a long period of time that it cannot even be measured. Another large unit of time is called a millennium. A millennium is the name we give to 1,000 years. Besides years, there are months, weeks, days, hours, minutes, and seconds.

Fractions of seconds

There are 12 months in a year, just over four weeks in a month, and seven days in a week. A day is divided into 24 hours, and one hour contains 60 minutes. There are 60 seconds in a minute. A second is made up of 1,000 milliseconds and 1,000 million (1,000,000,000) nanoseconds.

▼ Clocks measure time in hours, minutes, and seconds. This clock is an alarm clock. When the alarm goes off, the hammer at the top of the clock moves back and forth. It hits the bells to make a loud noise.

hammer

bell

HOW MUCH TIME?

Enter the missing periods of time in this list:

15 billion years = age of the Universe

4.5 billion years = age of Earth

80 years = average lifetime of a person

22 months = time it takes for a baby elephant to grow inside its mother

? months = the number of months in a year

? days = time it takes for Earth to circle the Sun

8 hours = amount of sleep most adults need

? seconds = the number of seconds in an hour

8 minutes = the time it takes for light to travel from the Sun to Earth

1 second = beat of a human heart

Answers on page 31.

▲ **Most people live for almost 80 years. As time passes, a baby grows into a child and then an adult.**

WORD BANK   **Millennium: a period of time that lasts for 1,000 years**

ANCIENT CLOCKS

Thousands of years ago, the ancient Egyptians invented sundials, which tell time using the Sun's position in the sky. When the Sun shines on the sundial, the pointer casts a shadow onto the dial (round face). The dial is marked with the hours, from one to twelve. As the Sun moves around the sky, the shadow moves around the dial, just like the hour hand of a clock.

▼ The sunrise at Stonehenge on the morning of June 21, the summer solstice.

▶ STONEHENGE

This great circle of stones at Stonehenge (right) in England is about 4,000 years old. Many people believe it is an ancient clock or calendar. On the day of the summer solstice (the longest day of the year), the Sun rises exactly in line with some of the stones. Ancient people could have used Stonehenge to tell when the solstice happened.

CANDLE CLOCK
As a candle clock burned down, people could count the number of hours that had passed.

HOURGLASS
It takes exactly one hour for the sand to trickle from the top to the bottom of this hourglass.

OIL CLOCK
People could tell the time using an oil clock by the amount of oil that burned away in the lamp.

EGYPTIAN WATER CLOCK
Water drips slowly from a hole in a pot and shows how many hours have passed.

▲ Some early ways to tell time.

Other ways to tell time

Sundials are not very accurate, so ancient people had to think of other ways to tell time. Some things always take the same amount of time to happen. In an hourglass, for example, it takes exactly one hour for a fixed amount of sand to trickle from the top half of the hourglass to the bottom half. People could measure each passing hour by turning over an hourglass.

WORD BANK *Summer solstice: day with the most daylight hours*

TRACKING TIME

▲ This circular stone is an ancient Aztec calendar. It is 12 feet (3.6 meters) across. The Aztecs lived in Mexico hundreds of years ago.

▶▶▶ **B**esides measuring the hours in a day, people also needed calendars to track the days in a year. Nearly 2,500 years ago, people who lived in Babylon (now part of Iraq) created the first calendars. They saw that the Moon took about 29.5 days to complete a cycle from one full Moon to another. They called this time a month.

A better calendar

Their year had 12 of these months, which gave a total of 354 days. Their calendar was not exact, though. A year really has 365 days.

Thousands of years ago, the ancient Egyptians made a better calendar using the Sun. They figured out how long Earth took to move around the Sun. They called that time a year.

The Egyptians divided their year into 12 to make the months. Each month had 30 days. The ancient Egyptians added five extra days at the end of the year to make a total of 365 days.

▶ TRY THIS

+ − = x + − = x + − = x + − = x +

READ A CALENDAR

On this calendar page, the days of the week are arranged in vertical columns. It shows that the third Monday in the month is January 16.

What is the date of the second Tuesday in the month? And what is the date of the third Friday?

Answers on page 31.

JANUARY						
MON	TUE	WED	THU	FRI	SAT	SUN
						1
2	3	4	5	6	7	8
9	10	11	12	13	14	15
(16)	17	18	19	20	21	22
23	24	25	26	27	28	29
30	31					

▲ This is the calendar page for January 2012.

+ − = x + − = x + − = x + − = x + − = − = x + − x

WORD BANK   *Month: the time it takes for the Moon to circle Earth*

SWINGING PENDULUMS

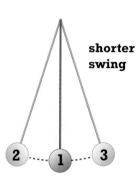

▶▶▶ **I**magine if you had to go outside to look at a sundial whenever you wanted to know the time, or if you had to fill up a water clock so you would be on time for school. Early clocks like these were not very useful.

In the 17th century, a famous Italian scientist named Galileo (1564–1642) invented the pendulum. A pendulum is a long bar with a heavy weight at one end.

Controlling a clock

If a pendulum is kept swinging, it always takes the same amount of time to swing back and forth. That makes a pendulum useful to help tell time.

▼ Each time a pendulum swings, it travels the same distance either side (2 and 3) of its starting point (1). As it slows, the pendulum swings less far, but the distance between 1 and 2 is always the same as the distance between 1 and 3.

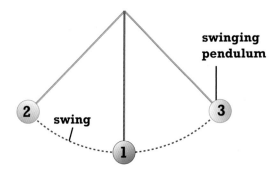

swinging pendulum

swing

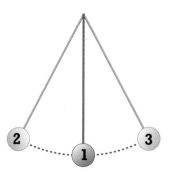

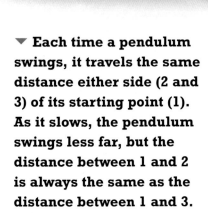

shorter swing

▶ **TRY THIS**   + − = x + − = x + −

SWINGING PENDULUMS

A complete pendulum swing is the time it takes to get back to its starting position (from 2 to 3 and back to 2 again in the diagrams on page 12).

If a pendulum makes a full swing once every 2 seconds, how many will it make in 1 minute?

If it takes 3 seconds to make a full swing, how many swings will it make in a minute?

Answers on page 31.

+ − = x + − = x + − = x + − = x + −

▲ A swing works in the same way as a pendulum. Like a pendulum, the girl will swing in a regular pattern.

Galileo

Galileo suggested using a swinging pendulum to control how a clock works. Gravity is the force that makes things fall toward Earth. It also keeps Earth and the other planets moving around the Sun. Gravity also makes a pendulum swing. Galileo was fascinated by gravity. He got the idea for the pendulum while he was watching a lamp swinging in the cathedral in Pisa, Italy. When he timed the swings using the pulse in his wrist, he found the lamp always took exactly the same time to move back and forth.

FACT

The world's biggest pendulum clock is in Japan. It is 95 feet (29 meters) tall.

WORD BANK   *Gravity: a force that pulls things toward Earth*

PENDULUM CLOCKS

Pendulum clocks are mechanical. They have lots of moving parts. Some of the most important parts are called gears—wheels with jagged teeth cut into their edges—that make a clock's hands turn. The swinging pendulum controls how fast the gears move. A slowly falling weight powers the clock. One problem is that the pendulum may change length slightly in hot or cold weather. That makes the clock run too fast or too slow.

Then, in the 15th century, clockmakers found another way to drive clocks. Instead of using a falling weight, they used springs. These little spirals of wire keep a clock ticking at an exact rate as they unwind.

◀ **An old pendulum clock.**

▶ THE MOVING PARTS

When a pendulum swings, it rocks a lever called a pallet. The pallet lifts up and down once every second. This makes a "tick-tock" noise. As the pallet moves, it turns the escape wheel. This wheel is connected by gears to other wheels, including the main wheel.

Falling weight

The main wheel has a heavy weight fixed to it that slowly moves down. The falling weight powers the clock by turning the main wheel. The main wheel then turns the other gears. The swinging pendulum controls the movement of the gears, which turn the hands around the dial. The clock has to be wound regularly to raise the weight back up to the barrel.

▶ The moving parts of a pendulum clock.

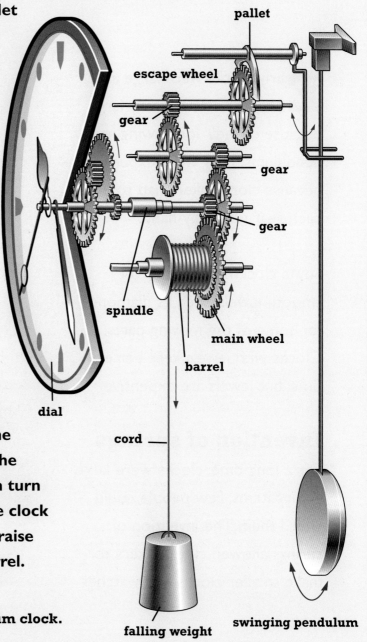

pallet

escape wheel

gear

gear

gear

spindle

main wheel

barrel

dial

cord

falling weight

swinging pendulum

WORD BANK *Mechanical clock: one that is made of moving parts*

CLOCKS AND WATCHES

Early clocks were large and expensive. They were large because of their long, swinging pendulums. They were expensive because clockmakers had to cut each gear wheel by hand.

Some clockmakers used very smooth jewels, such as diamonds, for some of the moving parts. Clocks with jewels kept better time, but jewels are expensive.

Invention of springs

For a long time, clocks were large luxury items. Few people could afford them. The invention of springs allowed clockmakers to make smaller clocks and watches

▶ This clockmaker is using an eyepiece to see the tiny parts in a watch.

► CLOCKS AT SEA

Early mechanical clocks were fine on land but could not be used on ships. The tumbling waves of the sea made it impossible for a pendulum to swing properly. A British clockmaker named John Harrison (1693–1776) solved the problem of how to tell time at sea. He built very accurate sea clocks driven by special springs. One was a large pocket watch. It lost only five seconds during a sea voyage from England to Jamaica in 1762.

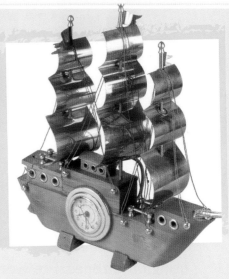

▲ This old sea clock told time accurately even on a ship that was rocking on a stormy ocean.

FACT

Some accurate modern watches have more than 200 parts crammed into a tiny space.

without pendulums and falling weights. In 1841, a British engineer named Joseph Whitworth (1803–1887) invented a machine that cut gears very precisely. This machine enabled people to make small clocks and watches far more quickly. Soon they could be made in factories.

These watches and clocks were less expensive, so many more people were able to buy them.

WORD BANK   *Gear: joined wheels with jagged teeth around their edges*

DIFFERENT TIMES AROUND THE WORLD

When you are having breakfast in the morning, somewhere else in the world, other people are having dinner. Everyone agrees what time it is using time zones. The world is divided into 24 time zones. People living in each zone have their own time.

Greenwich Mean Time

Everyone's time is set by the time at Greenwich in England. The time there is called Greenwich Mean Time (GMT). People living in time zones east of

▼ Earth as seen from the Moon. Only one side of Earth faces the Sun at any one time. It is daytime on the side that faces the Sun and nighttime on the other side. As Earth spins around, different parts face the Sun.

Greenwich have later times than GMT. People living in time zones west of Greenwich have earlier times.

Atlantic to Pacific

North America is such a big continent that it has five different time zones. The time is always three hours later in the day for New Yorkers than it is for Californians. That is because the Sun rises earlier over New York than over California.

▶ **TRY THIS**

WHAT TIME IS IT?

Look at the map below and work out the time in different places.

When it is 12 noon in New York City, what time is it in Los Angeles? When it is 4 p.m. in Los Angeles, what time is it in New York City? When it is 8 a.m. in New York City, what time is it in Florida?

Answers on page 31.

+ – = x + – = x + – = x + – =

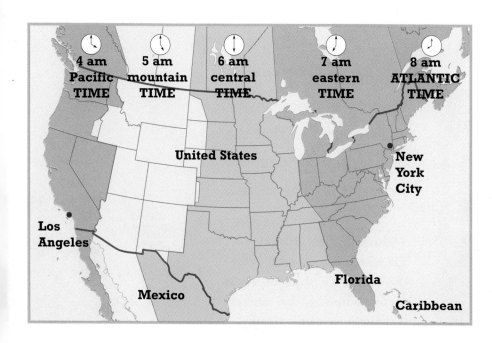

◀ **North America has five different time zones. When it is 7 a.m. in New York City, it is only 4 a.m. on the west coast in Los Angeles, California.**

WORD BANK   *Time zone: a region of Earth that has the same time*

TIME AND SPEED

▶▶▶ **W**hen you feel bored, time seems to pass slowly. When you are having fun, time seems to speed by. That is a trick of the mind—time almost always passes at the same speed. But a brilliant German-born American scientist named Albert Einstein (1879–1955) showed that sometimes time can speed up or slow down.

Traveling at the speed of light

Light travels at the incredibly fast speed of 186,000 miles (298,000 km) each second. Suppose you could sit on a beam of light and zoom along with it.

Einstein said that time would pass more slowly for you traveling on that beam of light than for people who were not moving so fast.

◀ **The scientist Albert Einstein. He showed that the faster an object travels through space, the slower it travels through time.**

Einstein also said that time passes more slowly as the pull of gravity gets stronger. So time passes slightly slower near the ground than it does in space, where the pull of Earth's gravity is less.

Einstein's ideas are called the theory of relativity and made people think about time and space in new ways.

◀ Time passes slightly faster on a rocket when it orbits Earth than it does on the ground.

▶ TRY THIS

SPEEDING LIGHT

Can you solve these problems? Remember that in 1 second, light travels 186,000 miles (298,000 km).

How far will light travel in 10 seconds? How far will it travel in 1 minute? How long will a beam of light take to travel from a star 3,720,000 miles (5,960,000 km) away?

Answers on page 31.

GREAT PERIODS OF TIME

▶▶▶ **C**locks measure the hours in a day. Calendars help us keep track of the months and years. How can we measure even longer periods of time? Suppose scientists want to know how old a fossil is. A fossil is the remains of a long-dead creature that has turned to stone. No clock will tell them.

American chemist William Libby (1908–1980) discovered the answer in 1947. He found that

HOW A FOSSIL FORMS

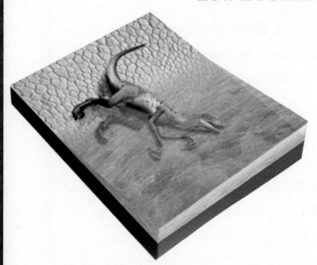

1. Millions of years ago, a dinosaur dies next to a river.

2. The dinosaur's flesh rots, until only the bones are left. The river covers these bones in mud.

he could figure out how old something was by measuring how much of a certain kind of carbon it contained. Libby called this method carbon dating. It works for things that are up to 60,000 years old.

Fossils and rocks

Carbon dating does not work for fossils that are millions of years old. For these, radioactive elements are now used to tell us their ages.

Everything that has ever lived contains some carbon. It is the black material in coal and in pencil "lead." Over thousands of years, one kind of carbon changes into another kind of carbon. The change happens very slowly but at a steady rate. The changing carbon in living or dead things is like a slowly ticking clock. By measuring the different amounts of carbon present, a scientist can figure out how old something is.

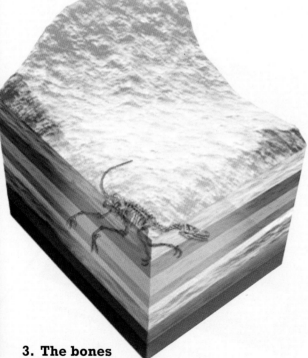

3. The bones are covered by layers of rocks over millions of years. The bones turn into stone.

4. The fossil is found when the rocks wear away. Scientists then use a process called radiometric dating to work out how old it is.

WORD BANK *Carbon dating: a way of finding out the age of very old things*

MODERN CLOCKS

Modern clocks and watches are not powered by falling weights or springs. They run on batteries, or electric power. A tiny battery makes the electricity to keep the watch going. Some clocks and watches use a tiny piece of quartz to tell the time. Quartz is a type of crystal. When electricity flows into it, the crystal shakes back and forth at a precise rate. Quartz watches use this shaking movement to keep track of the time.

▶ **This modern cell phone has a digital time display (showing the time is 12:56) and an alarm that will go off at 8 a.m.**

FACT

Pure quartz has another name: silicon dioxide. It is made of atoms of silicon and oxygen.

Some people tell time with watches and clocks that have moving hands. Others prefer digital clocks and watches. Digital clocks show the time with numbers, or digits. They often have a built-in stopwatch and alarm clock. Some watches may also show the time in different countries. Inside a digital watch, there is usually a piece of quartz crystal to keep time.

Digital displays

It takes very little energy to make quartz move. So the battery in a quartz watch can last for many years. The first quartz clock was made in 1928 by American engineers Joseph Horton and Warren Marrison. The first quartz wristwatch was launched in Japan in 1969, though it was very expensive. Three years later, the Hamilton Watch Company of Pennsylvania produced the first watch with a digital display. The first watches that could download information from computers went on sale in the 1990s.

▲ **This boy is using a digital stopwatch to time how long it takes to do something.**

MORE CLOCKS

nce people told time by looking at the skies. In the last few hundred years, clockmakers have found much better methods of measuring time. These methods include pendulums and weights, spring-driven clocks, and digital watches. How will people tell time in the future?

▼ **This navigation unit has a display that tells a driver a car's location. The digital display also shows the time and how long the driver has been on the road.**

Most accurate

The most accurate way of telling time now is with an atomic clock. An atomic clock works like a superaccurate quartz clock. Instead of quartz, an atomic clock uses atoms, particles so small we cannot see them. These atoms

FACT

The kurinji plant has a slow-running biological clock. It flowers only once every 12 years.

BIOLOGICAL CLOCKS

We all have a built-in sense of time. Even without looking at a clock, we know when we feel sleepy or hungry. That is called our biological clock. Scientists think our biological clocks are driven by proteins. Proteins are the chemicals from which our bodies are made. In the future, scientists are sure to find out much more about biological clocks.

▶ Flowers bloom only at certain times of year. This is a kind of biological clock.

give off pulses of energy ten billion times every second. The clock counts these pulses to work out and show the time.

Atomic wristwatches?

Atomic clocks are extremely accurate. One that was built in 2011 will lose just one second every 138 million years. Perhaps in the future we will all wear atomic watches on our wrists. There would be no excuse for missing classes!

WORD BANK   *Atom: a very tiny particle of a substance*

MAKE A SUNDIAL

YOU WILL NEED

- **A piece of thin cardboard about 12 inches (30 cm) by 12 inches (30 cm)**
- **A sharp pencil**
- **A dinner plate about 10 inches (25 cm) across**
- **Modeling clay**
- **Scissors**

WHAT TO DO

1. Put the plate on top of the cardboard. Draw around the edge of the plate to make a circle on the cardboard.

2. Cut out the circle using the scissors. Get an adult to help you. Be very careful with the scissors.

3. Figure out roughly where the center of the circle is. Make a small pencil mark there.

4. Put a small ball of modeling clay on the underside of the cardboard beneath the pencil mark.

5. Carefully push the pencil through the center of the cardboard so it goes through the modeling clay. Ask an adult to help you. Try not to bend the cardboard.

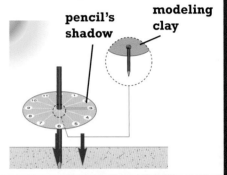

Your finished sundial

Once you have drawn the hour lines for 3, 6, 9, and 12 o'clock, you can figure out where the other hour lines go by dividing each quarter of the circle into equal thirds.

pencil's shadow

modeling clay

6. Place your sundial on the ground outside. Choose somewhere that will be in sunshine all day.

7. At noon, draw a straight line where the pencil's shadow falls. Do the same at 3 o'clock and 6 o'clock in the afternoon, and at 9 o'clock in the morning.

GLOSSARY

atom A tiny particle of a substance.

atomic clock A very accurate clock that tells time using the tiny movements of atoms.

biological clock An animal's or plant's built-in sense of time.

calendar A way of keeping track of the days, weeks, and months in a year.

carbon dating A way of finding out the age of very old things.

digital watch A watch that shows the time with numbers, not hands.

escape wheel The main driving wheel in a pendulum clock.

gear A pair of interlocking wheels with teeth around their edges. The wheels turn at different speeds depending on how many teeth each has.

gravity A force that pulls things toward Earth.

mechanical clock A clock that is made of moving parts, such as gears, pendulums, and springs.

millennium A period of time that lasts for 1,000 years.

month The approximate time it takes for the Moon to go once around Earth.

pendulum A swinging bar that helps keep time in a mechanical clock.

quartz clock A modern clock that uses the tiny vibrations of the mineral quartz (silicon dioxide) to keep time.

relativity A theory of the great scientist Albert Einstein; in relativity, time slows down when people travel at very high speeds.

summer solstice The day of the year with the most daylight hours (around June 21). The winter solstice (around December 22) has the fewest daylight hours of any day in the year.

spring A spiral of wire that powers a mechanical clock.

sundial A device that measures time using shadows.

time zone A region of the world that has the same time.

year The time it takes for Earth to move once around the Sun (365 days).

FIND OUT MORE

BOOKS

Thomas and Heather Adamson, **How Do You Measure Time?** Mankato, MN: Capstone, 2011.

Penny Dowdy, **Time.** New York: Crabtree, 2009.

Sally Hewitt, **Time: What Is It?** Mankato, MN: Stargazer, 2008.

Dana Meachen Rau, **Space and Time.** New York: Marshall Cavendish Benchmark, 2008.

WEBSITES

Interactive clock
Change the time on an interactive clock face and convert times to digital.
http://www.time-for-time.com/swf/myclox.swf

Telling Time Games for Kids
Online activities with clocks.
http://www.free-training-tutorial.com/telling-time -games.html

Publisher's note to educators and parents: Our editors have carefully reviewed these websites to ensure that they are suitable for students. Many websites change frequently, however, and we cannot guarantee that a site's future contents will continue to meet our high standards of quality and educational value. Be advised that students should be closely supervised whenever they access the Internet.

Answers to questions
Page 7: There are 12 months in a year; there are 365 days in a year (366 every fourth, or leap, year); and there are 3,600 seconds in an hour (60 seconds in a minute and 60 minutes in an hour; 60 x 60 = 3,600).
Page 11: The second Tuesday on the calendar is January 10; the third Friday is January 20.
Page 13: The first pendulum will make 30 swings in a minute; the second pendulum will make 20 swings in a minute.
Page 19: When it is 12 noon in New York, it is 9 a.m. in Los Angeles; when it is 4 p.m. in Los Angeles it is 7 p.m. in New York; when it is 8 a.m. in New York it is also 8 a.m. in Florida.
Page 21: In 10 seconds, light will travel 1,860,000 miles (2,980,000 km); in 1 minute, light will travel 11,160,000 miles (17,880,000 km); it will take 20 seconds for light to travel from the star.

INDEX